TABLE OF CONTENTS

INTRODUCTION

The sailors keep quiet. The **sonar** technician has just alerted the captain to a nearby unauthorized **vessel**. Seconds tick . . . tick . . . tick. The two vessels are in a tense standoff. Finally, a voice breaks the silence. "All clear," says the sonar technician. The other ship has turned away from the protected waters. The sailors quickly get back to work. These sailors are busy protecting U.S. interests on the seas. Few would dare engage them.

The United States Navy began in 1775 during the American Revolutionary War (1775–1783). At first, it was a temporary force. It wasn't until 1794 that the Navy was officially re-established. Pirates were attacking U.S. **merchant** ships. The Navy has been protecting the country at sea ever since.

Today, the U.S. Navy has around 330,000 **active duty** members. These sailors serve as engineers, chefs, information specialists, and more. More than 150 different careers are part of the Navy. They help make the U.S. Navy what it is.

Over the years, many have served. Many have died. All should be honored.

DISCOVER "ANCHORS AWEIGH"

A Tribute to the U.S. Navy

Cherry Lake Press

Published in the United States of America by Cherry Lake Publishing
Ann Arbor, Michigan
www.cherrylakepublishing.com

Reading Adviser: Beth Walker Gambro, MS, Ed., Reading Consultant, Yorkville, IL

Photo Credits: PO2 Kenneth Lagadi/DVIDS/Public Domain, cover, title page; Department of Defense/Flickr, 5; Detroit Publishing Company photograph collection/Prints and Photographs Division/Library of Congress, 7; Department of Defense/Flickr, 8; Commander Andrew H. Foote, Public domain, via Wikimedia Commons, 9; Department of Defense/Flickr, 10; Department of Defense/Flickr, 11; PO1 Brian Glunt/DVIDS/Public Domain, 12; Courtesy Photo/DVIDS/Public Domain, 13; U.S. Navy photo by Mass Communication Specialist 2nd Class James R. Evans, Public domain, via Wikimedia Commons, 14; Timothy E Heaps/DVIDS/Public Domain, 15; Department of Veteran Affairs,16; SCPO Peter Lawlor/DVIDS/Public Domain, 17; PO1 John Bellino/DVIDS/Public Domain, 18; PO1 Jasen MorenoGarcia/DVIDS/Public Domain, 19; Department of Defense/Flickr, 20; SN Desiree Green/DVIDS/Public Domain, 21

Cherry Lake Press is an imprint of Cherry Lake Publishing Group

Library of Congress Cataloging-in-Publication Data has been filed and is available at catalog.loc.gov.

Cherry Lake Publishing Group would like to acknowledge the work of the Partnership for 21st Century Learning, a Network of Battelle for Kids. Please visit Battelle for Kids online for more information.

Printed in the United States of America

Note from Publisher: Websites change regularly, and their future contents are outside of our control. Supervise children when conducting any recommended online searches for extended learning opportunities.

"ANCHORS AWEIGH"

The song "Anchors Aweigh" is the unofficial song of the U.S. Navy. The song was first performed in 1906. The music was written by Charles A. Zimmermann. The lyrics were written by Midshipman Alfred H. Miles.

Stand Navy out to sea,
Fight our battle cry;

★ **NAVY FACTS** "Hooyah!" is a **rallying cry** for Navy sailors. It started with Navy Sea, Air, and Land (SEAL) teams. They have special training. "Hooyah!" likely came from a training exercise. The Navy SEALs were exhausted. But they yelled "Hooyah!" to keep going.

We'll never change our course,
So vicious foe steer shy-y-y-y.

LOOK

Look at this historical image of Navy sailors. How are the uniforms different from modern uniforms you see in this book?

★ **NAVY FACTS** Some "vicious foe" of the Navy are pirates. Navy sailors have fought pirates since the early 1800s. And they still do in modern times! Pirates held American Captain Richard Phillips **hostage** in 2009. Navy SEALS saved him.

Roll out the TNT,

★ **NAVY FACTS** Many types of ships are used in the U.S. Navy. Some are aircraft carriers, cruisers, and destroyers. Others are submarines, **amphibious** craft, and combat ships. The Navy also has hospital ships. These ships provide medical support.

Anchors Aweigh.

★ **NAVY FACTS** The **transatlantic** slave trade was declared illegal in the United States in 1807. The U.S. Navy began its African Slave Trade Patrol in 1819. They stopped and captured ships trying to illegally move enslaved peoples to the United States.

Sail on to victory
And sink their bones to Davy Jones, hooray!

ASK QUESTIONS

Why do you think the Navy doesn't have an official motto? Do some digging to find the answer.

★ **NAVY FACTS** An unofficial Navy **motto** is *Non sibi sed patriae*. This is Latin for "Not self, but country." This phrase shows sailors' commitment to selflessly serve their country.

Anchors Aweigh, my boys,
Anchors Aweigh.

★ **NAVY FACTS** The Navy uses different terms for everyday things. Ship walls are called "bulkheads." Left is "port." Right is "starboard." Windows are "portholes." The bathroom is the "head." Mopping is "swabbing."

Farewell to foreign shores,
We sail at break of day-ay-ay-ay.

★ **NAVY FACTS** Sailors line up along the deck to honor people and places. This is called manning the rail. They do this when leaving ports at home and abroad, when passing memorials, and for world leaders.

Through our last night ashore,
Drink to the foam,

MAKE A GUESS

How many active submarines do you think are part of the U.S. Navy? Make a guess! Then research to find out if you're right.

★ **NAVY FACTS** Sailors don't often get to choose where they are stationed. Submarine sailors often work long shifts in small spaces. It is extra tough work. So any sailor serving on a submarine specifically volunteers for that duty.

Until we meet once more.

"It follows then as certain as that night succeeds the day, that without a decisive naval force we can do nothing definitive, and with it, everything honorable and glorious."
– President George Washington, November 15, 1781

Here's wishing you a happy voyage home.

★ **NAVY FACTS** It's not all about fighting! Sailors have a long history of helping people in need. They assist with disaster relief. They rescue people at sea. They help refugees. They offer medical aid in emergency situations.

Blue of the mighty deep:
Gold of God's great sun.

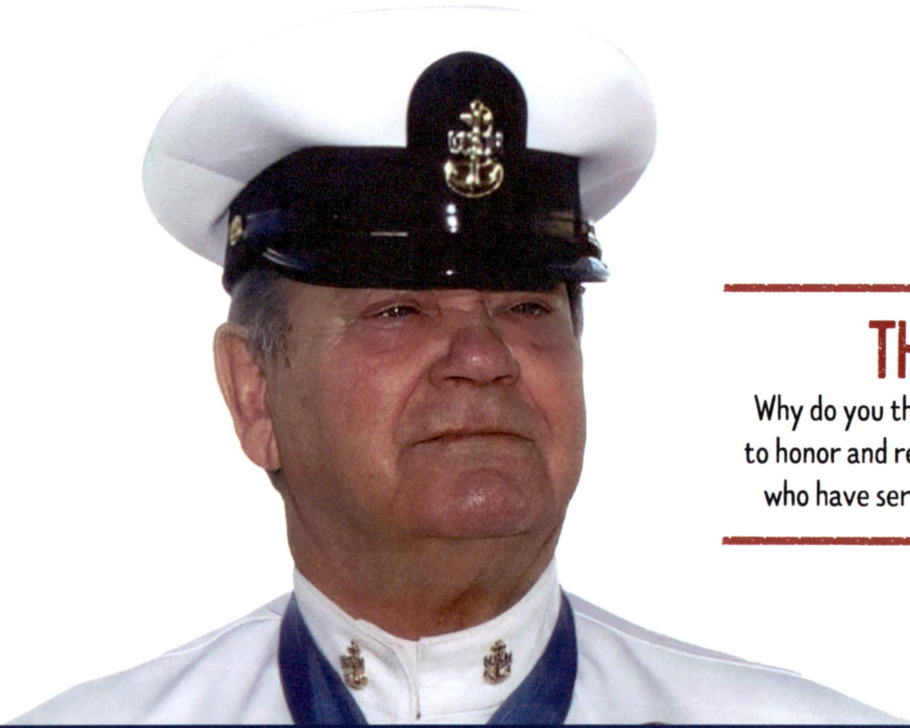

THINK

Why do you think it's important to honor and respect Navy sailors who have served our country?

★ **NAVY FACTS** Chief Petty Officer James E. Williams (1930–1999) was a Navy sailor. He is the most decorated sailor in Navy history. He served for 20 years and earned 15 individual awards. They include a Navy Cross for **heroism** in combat.

Let these our colors be
Till all of time be done, done, done, done.

★ **NAVY FACTS** The U.S. Naval Academy has a mascot named Bill the Goat. Legend has it that there was once a Navy ship with a pet goat named Bill. He passed away. The sailors saved the skin. They ran around a Naval Academy football game wearing it. A mascot was born.

On seven seas we learn
Navy's stern call:

★ **NAVY FACTS** Millions of people are Navy **veterans**. Of all U.S. military veterans, about 21 percent served in the U.S. Navy. Those who served are Navy sailors for life and are forever honored for their service.

Faith, courage, service true,

★ **NAVY FACTS** The U.S. Navy has 69 active bases at home and abroad. The United States is home to 57 of them. California and Florida have the most. There are 10 bases in California. There are eight in Florida. There are also 12 overseas.

"The Navy has both a tradition and a future—and we look with pride and confidence in both directions."

– Admiral George Anderson, August 1, 1961

With honor, over honor, over all.

CREATE

Research one of the active Navy vessels. Draw a diagram and label what each area of the ship is for. Include a list of jobs sailors do in the different areas. What skills do sailors need for those jobs? Share what you learned.

THE SAILOR'S CREED

I am a United States Sailor.

I will support and defend the Constitution
of the United States of America
and I will obey the orders of
those appointed over me.

I represent the fighting spirit of the Navy
and those who have gone before me
to defend freedom and democracy
around the world.

I proudly serve my country's Navy combat
team with Honor, Courage
and Commitment.

I am committed to excellence and
the fair treatment of all.

LEARN MORE

BOOKS

Bolte, Mari. *Life in the U.S. Navy*. North Mankato, MN: Capstone, 2024.

Bolte, Mari. *Warships in Action*. Minneapolis, MN: Lerner, 2024.

Miller, Marie-Therese. *Strong Submarines*. Minneapolis, MN: Lerner, 2025.

WEBSITES

Search these online sources with an adult.

Anchors Aweigh – with lyrics – US Navy Song | Music & Lyrics via YouTube

United States Navy Facts for Kids | Kiddle

GLOSSARY

active duty (AK-tiv DOO-tee) describing a member of the U.S. Armed Forces who works for the military full-time and can be deployed

amphibious (am-FIH-bee-uhs) adapted for both water and land

Davy Jones (DAY-vee JOHNZ) short for "Davy Jones's Locker;" term for the bottom of the sea

heroism (HER-uh-wih-zuhm) great bravery

hostage (HAH-stij) person taken by force until a taker's demands are met

merchant (MUHR-chuhnt) describing something a trader uses to buy and sell goods for profit

motto (MAH-toh) short expression or guiding principle

rallying cry (RAA-lee-ing KRIE) shouted word, phrase, or sound used to excite or rouse people

sonar (SOH-nahr) device for detecting and locating objects underwater

TNT (tee-en-TEE) a powerful explosive; abbreviation for trinitrotoluene

transatlantic (trans-uht-LAN-tik) involving crossing the Atlantic Ocean

vessel (VEH-suhl) watercraft that is larger than a rowboat

veterans (VEH-tuh-ruhnz) former members of the armed forces

INDEX